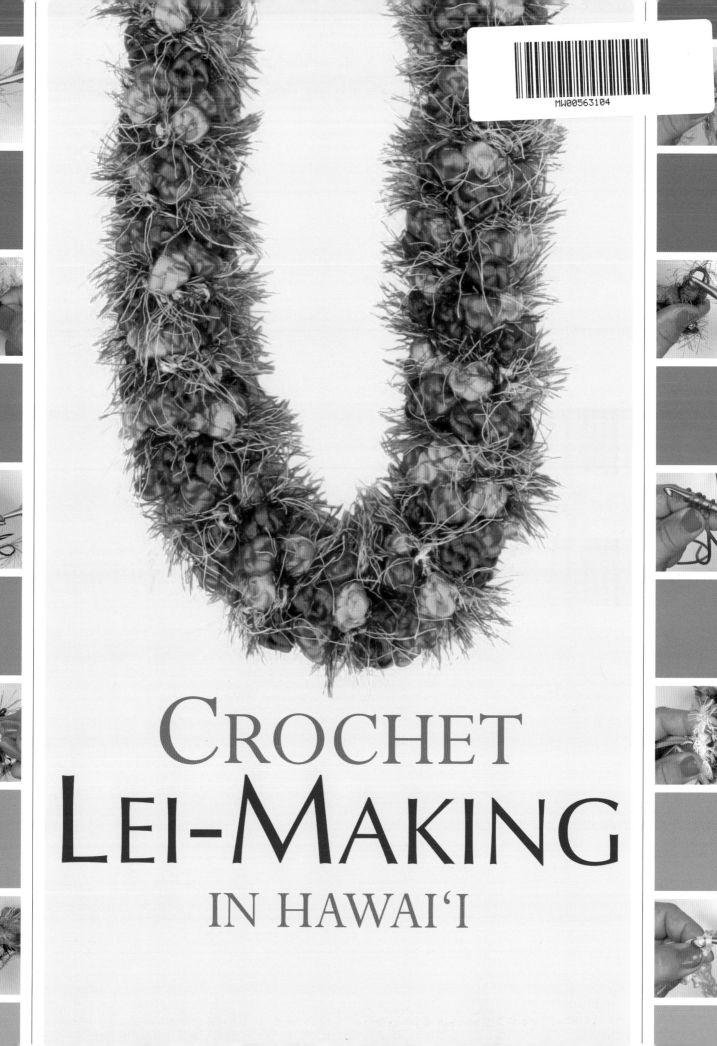

CROCHET
LEI-MAKING
IN HAWAI'I

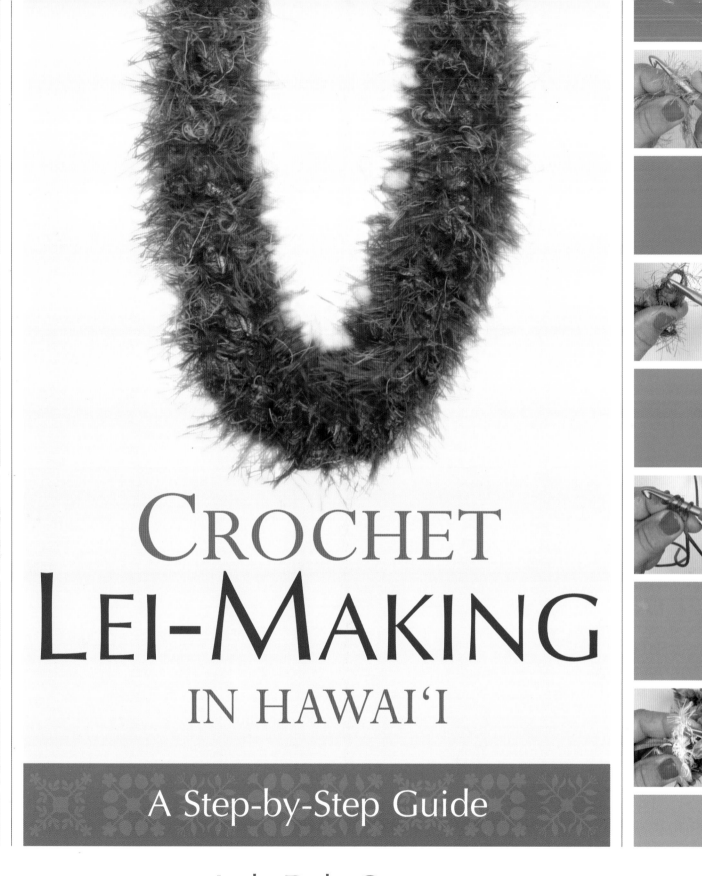

CROCHET
LEI-MAKING
IN HAWAI'I

Judy Dela Cruz

MUTUAL PUBLISHING

ISBN-10: 1-56647-717-4
ISBN-13: 978-1-56647-717-8

Library of Congress Catalog Card Number: 2005922867

Design by Emily R. Lee

First Printing, May 2005
Second Printing, February 2007
2 3 4 5 6 7 8 9

Mutual Publishing, LLC
1215 Center Street, Suite 210
Honolulu, Hawai'i 96816
Ph: 808-732-1709 / Fax: 808-734-4094
email: info@mutualpublishing.com
www.mutualpublishing.com

Printed in Korea

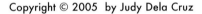

Mahalo to:

The Lord for giving me my craftiness.

My husband, Leonard, for encouraging me.

My granddaughter, Cheryl Gonsalves, for all her help.

My sons, Tommy and Terry.

Laurie Ide for convincing me to write this book.

Jana Jones for her great support and advice.

Marlene Costa for the use of her hands.

Lynette Espirito for her wonderful advice and support.

Also to everyone who supports me by buying this book.

Mahalo to all of you and hope you have fun with it.

Good Luck!!

Table of Contents

Crochet lei-making is a rewarding experience. It's not just a hobby, but a way to express yourself and share your aloha. Use your imagination to create your own lei. Look at all the many flowers in Hawai'i—from bougainvillea to lehua—then combine colors and textures using various yarns to create those flowers. You can have a lot of fun with this.

If you don't know how to crochet, no problem. I have taught women who never picked up a crochet needle to make these lei. The stitches used to make the lei in this book are basic stitches—single crochet and chains. Practice with a simple, clean yarn and you'll be surprised how easy it is.

Remember, there's no wrong way to make a lei. Every lei is different because every person making it is different. Let your personality come through, and have fun.

I have been crocheting since I was a teenager. I learned on my own from a beginner's crochet book. Soon I was crocheting shawls, sweaters, baby booties, and more. I was amazed at the amount of things I could create with different types of yarns.

About three years ago, someone showed me their crochet lei, and I just had to learn to make them. The very next morning, I had my husband take me to Yarn & Needle Crafts in Kailua and began to crochet the lei you can find in this book. They are all very easy to make. I have a friend, Debbie, who has never crocheted. She came to my home, and I had her begin simply by crocheting chains and single crochets. In no time at all she was making beautiful, ornate lei.

Anyone can crochet these beautiful lei, even a beginner. Photographic step-by-step instructions are given, making it easy to follow. For the advanced or intermediate crocheter, this book provides new designs and inspiration for you to create your own. Two basic stitches are used throughout this book—the single crochet and chain stitch. Just these two simple stitches will create beautiful lei such as the Hinahina (see page 21) and the 'Ohai Ali'i (see page 24). It all comes together with the types of ribbons and yarns used.

A list of supplies is provided for each lei. There are so many varieties and colors of yarn and ribbon that a photograph of each individual strand is provided to help you identify them. Take this book shopping with you so you know what to look for. Keep in mind that the sales staff at many of the Island's craft stores are very knowledgeable and can help you identify and find the correct yarns. But remember, you can be creative. Change the color of the yarns to fit your vision of the lei. For the Graduation Lei (see page 20), choose your school colors and you'll have a memento that will be treasured forever. I usually try to match the color of the lei to the flowers I am trying to create. That way it looks more natural.

It's amazing what you can do with ribbons and yarns. There is an incredibly wide variety out on the market today. The yarns used to make these lei were originally used to make sweaters and scarves, even hats. By using your imagination you can make anything with these yarns.

Just to name a few types of yarns, there's boa, eyebrow, eyelash, fizz, mustache or mustachio. There are all kinds of brand names. You can purchase any of these yarns at any craft or department store that carries craft yarns. All you have to do is ask them if they have yarns used to make crocheted lei. You can experiment with any type of yarn. You may even create a new style of lei!

Just like the yarns, there are different sizes and types of ribbons. I like to use satin ribbon, but grosgrain ribbon can also be used. I use the 1/8-inch satin ribbon for my lead lines (lines you crochet on) and 5/8-inch satin ribbon for ending the lei.

When making your lei the most popular length is a short choker, which measures about 36 to 38 inches (120 loops). Then you have a lei po'o or head lei. These measurements differ depending on your head size. The lei po'o (125 to 130 loops) can also be used on a hat. Then there's your normal lei length, which measures 38 to 42 inches (250 to 300 loops).

Kukui nuts are the basic nuts I use to secure my lei when ending it, but you can use any variety of nuts to secure your lei, like sheep's eye, ironwood, Hawaiian gray pearl, and the blue marble. It just depends on how you want your final lei to look.

Do not worry about making mistakes. Everyone does, and it may not be noticeable; but if it is, I suggest you take it apart and correct it. Keep in mind that even the best crocheters may not notice it. The aloha you put into making the lei is much more important than how perfect the finished product it.

As I was creating some of my lei, my granddaughter, Cheryl, typed and saved all the directions on the computer. I suggest you also document your steps in making a lei—especially ones you create yourself. Maybe someone will want you to make a second lei, and this way you'll know what color yarns and ribbons you used. Keep a strand of each in a labeled bag or envelope, or keep the label from the yarns so you have something to refer.

Most of all, have fun, be creative, and be generous. A lei—whether it's made with flowers or with yarn and ribbon—is always made with aloha and should be given to and shared with others.

Supplies

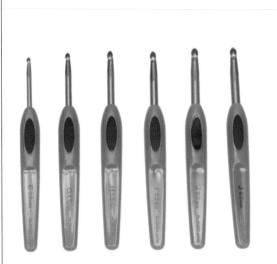

1 Crochet hook: I like to use the "J" hook, but it depends if your hand is tight or loose. If your hand is tight then it's best if you use a larger needle, but if your hand is loose then you should use a smaller needle. Try both, if you can, and see which feels more comfortable to you.

2 Ribbons: You can use satin or grosgrain ribbon. I use the satin ribbon because it is soft. I use 1/8-inch satin for making rosettes and pīkake. This book will show you when to use what kind and size ribbon. I also use 5/8-inch satin ribbon for ending the lei.

3 Yarns: There are so many different kinds of yarns for you to use and experiment with. Just to name a few there's: funny yarn (eyebrow), fizz (whiskers), peluche (mustache), salsa (eyebrow), and boa. When beginning, just pick up the type you need. After you've made a few lei and feel comfortable, experiment and see what you come up with by using different types of yarn. Pretty soon you'll be an expert and will know the difference between a fizz yarn and a boa yarn.

Crocheting is a very simple art—not only in how it's done, but what is needed. Basically, all you need is a needle and some yarn.

Locally, supplies can be found at Yarn & Needle Crafts on Oʻahu or on Maui. The staff is very helpful. All you have to do is say what lei you want to make, and they'll go and pull out the threads you need.

Any department store that carries crafts may also carry yarns. Stores like Ben Franklin, Honolulu Craft Supply, and WalMart are great places for yarns and threads. You can also look in the yellow pages under yarns or crafts. The internet is also a great resource. If you live on the mainland, the stores that carry the yarns used for these lei include Michaels, Hancock fabrics, or most other places that sell yarn.

Each lei in the book has a supply list telling you what yarns or ribbons are needed. A photograph is included to help you with identification. Measurements vary depending on what type of lei you want to make, so in terms of how much yarn or ribbon to purchase, I would suggest buying one ball of each. Two to three lei can be made from each ball of yarn or ribbon. As you make the different lei, you will begin to collect different colors and types of yarns and ribbons. Use your leftovers to create different colored lei. Although it may seem the supplies are expensive, remember that a number of lei can be made from one roll.

BASIC STITCHES AND PATTERNS

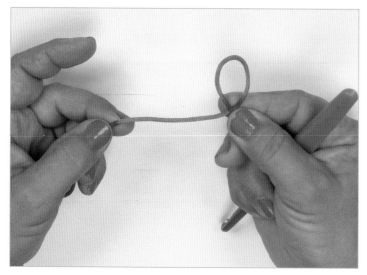

This is a basic crochet stitch that creates a chain of loops. This chain can be used as the first row of your lei—the foundation upon which other rows are built.

1 Draw up a loop with your yarn.

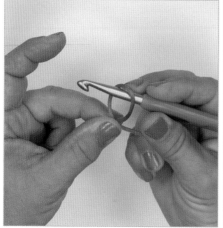

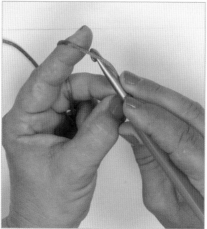

2 Pull your needle through the loop.

3 Hook the side of the yarn with your needle.

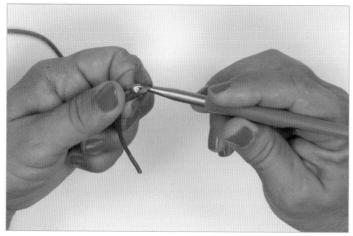

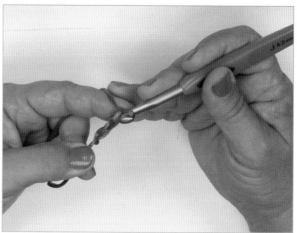

4 Pull the yarn through the loop.

5 Repeat the above steps to create a chain of yarn.

Single Crochet Stitch

This is a basic crochet stitch that is built on a foundation of chains or a lead line of ribbon.

1 Make a foundation row of chains or use your lead line of ribbon.

2 Insert hook through the first chain (if using ribbon: ribbon over hook).

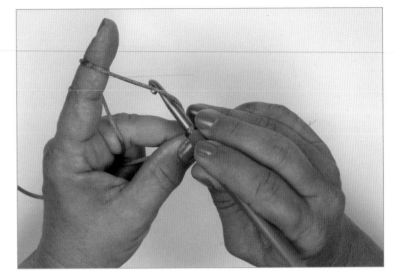

3 Yarn over hook.

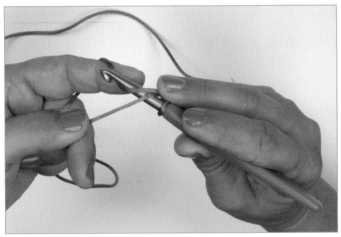

4 Pull through the first chain. If using ribbon, pull hook under the ribbon.

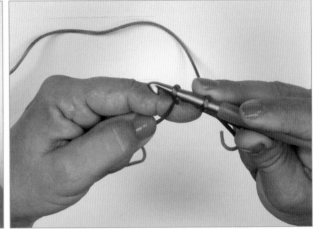

5 There will be two loops of yarn on your hook.

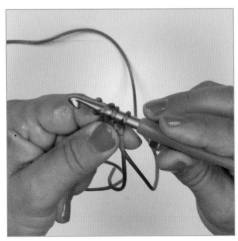 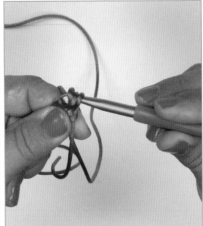 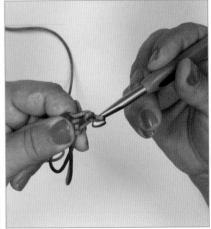

6 Yarn over and pull through the two loops.

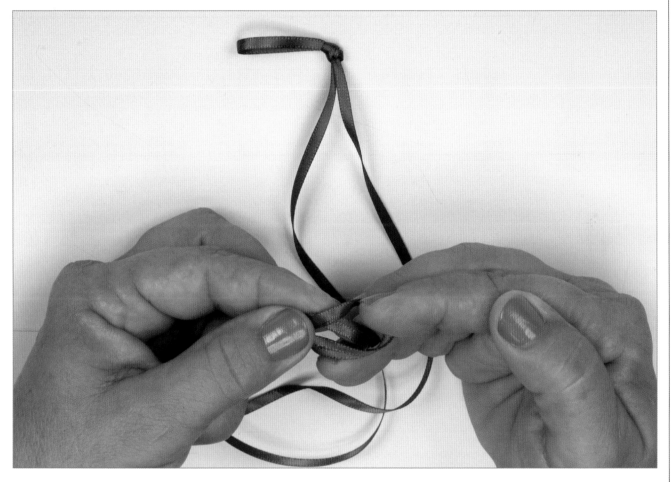

To begin your lei you need a lead line. You can make lei any length you choose, but the two common lengths referred to in this book are the choker length and the regular length.

For a choker length lei: Measure 1/8-inch ribbon (any color will do) about 60 inches. Fold the ribbon in half (30 inches) then tie a knot at both ends to secure the lei from sliding off the line.

For a regular length lei: Measure 1/8-inch ribbon (any color will do) about 100 inches. Fold the ribbon in half (50 inches) then tie a knot at both ends to secure the lei from sliding off the line.

Crochet Lei Pattern #1

Supplies:
See the instructions in the second half of this book for supplies specific to the lei you choose.

1 Make a loop with your yarn.

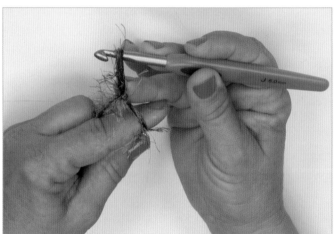

2 Pull the yarn through the loop.

3 Take your lead line (see page 3) and single crochet in between ribbons, then chain 3.

4 First Row: Single crochet both ribbons together, then chain 3, and repeat until you have 125 loops. This is your first row. Single crochet into the last single crochet and do one more chain, pull through chain, and cut off threads.

5 Second Row: Single crochet both ribbons together. Chain 3 in between loops. Repeat until the end of the row and end as row 1.

6 Single crochet both ribbons together and chain 3. Push 1st and 2nd single crochet to the right and single crochet, then chain 3 next to second single crochet. Repeat until the end of the row. End row same as rows 1 and 2.

7 Pull threads down to one end making sure you do not make it tight or your lei will look crooked. Tie the other end close to the last stitches.

Crochet Lei Pattern #2

Supplies:
J hook
Moss Green eyebrow
Gold Brown eyebrow
Brazilla #0074 eyebrow

There are so many lei you can create by changing the colors or threads. For instance, pīkake with off-white, and Pakalana with greens and oranges. Use your imagination! Find a book with flowers and match your yarn to the colors of the flowers.

This is a very easy lei to make. Using a J hook, all you do is chain 6 yards of double thread. When done, measure in half and half again until you have the desired length of strands. This is an easy beginner's lei.

1 Make a loop with your yarn.

2 Yarn over hook and pull through to form a chain stitch.

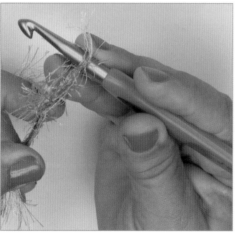

3 Chain stitch completed.

4 Continue chaining until you reach the desired length (about 6 yards).

5 Take 6 yards of lei and divide in half (3 yards) and then in half again.

6 Tie off the lei. You should have six strands of lei. Add a ribbon to hold the lei together.

6

1 Take your lead line (see page 3) and follow steps 1 and 2 on page 4. Then single crochet.

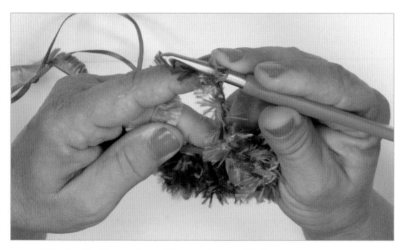

2 Chain 3. Repeat until you have 50 loops.

Supplies:

Two skeins of main color (Blue boa)
One skein of second color (White boa)
J hook

Graduation Lei

Choose the colors of your school and use any type of yarn. I prefer splash or boa to get the satin lei look.

- First color: Single crochet and chain 3 50 times, then cut off thread.
- Second color: Single crochet and chain 3 25 times, then cut off thread.

Repeat until length has been reached. I use 10 first color sections and 10 second color sections. End by tying lei together and add a bow.

This is one of the easiest lei to make. Use two colors of yarn one strand at a time. There are so many designs you can make. Just use your imagination and have fun with it.

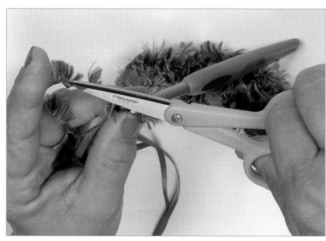

3 Snip off the yarn.

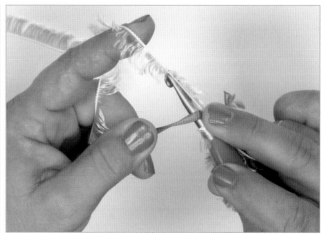

4 Attach a white or second color yarn.

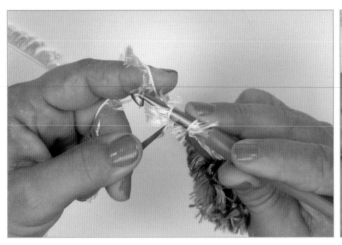

5 Single crochet and chain 3. Repeat until you have 25 loops.

6 Repeat, alternating blue and white yarn until you reach your desired length.

7 Tie the completed lei together. Add a bow where the ends join.

1 1st Row: Using your first two threads, single crochet in between 1/8-inch ribbons, chain 3.

Supplies needed:
Dark Blue 1/8-inch ribbon
Medium Blue 1/8-inch ribbon
Light Blue 1/8-inch ribbon
Olive eyebrow
Sherbert (fizz) whiskers
J hook

Rosettes or Pīkake

See the instructions in the second half of this book for supplies specific to the lei you choose.

Measure 60 inches of 1/8-inch ribbon (for choker), fold in half as in lei pattern #1. Tie both ends with a knot.

2 Single crochet, then chain 3 on line making sure you have 125 loops for choker-length, longer if making a regular lei.

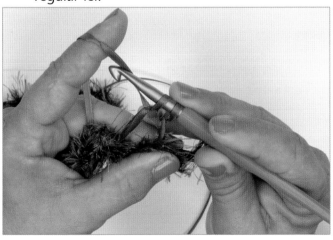 

3 2nd Row: Single crochet in between loops picking up both ribbons. Chain 4 and single crochet in 3rd chain from hook, single crochet in last chain, then chain 2.

4 Single crochet, then chain 4. Then single crochet in 3rd chain from hook. Single crochet in last chain, then chain 2. Repeat between loops. This will make 125 rosettes.

5 3rd Row: Using the first color ribbon, single crochet between loops and follow instructions for Row 1.

6 Chain 4 and single crochet in third chain from hook. Then single crochet in last chain.

7 Continue in between loops. Be sure to push greens and first ribbon to the right.

8 4th Row: using the second color ribbon, push 2 single crochet to the right.

9 Single crochet and chain 3 next to 2nd single crochet—follow directions for Row 2 to make rosettes.

10 Repeat until the end of the row. If you want to make a pīkake lei, use 1/8-inch ribbon or off-white 1/8-inch ribbon for all 3 rows or mix it with other color rosettes. To finish, see Ending Your Lei on page 15.

Supplies needed:
J hook
Red Rattail cord
Red Shiny Matical yarn (cellophane)

See the instructions in the second half of this book for supplies specific to the lei you choose.

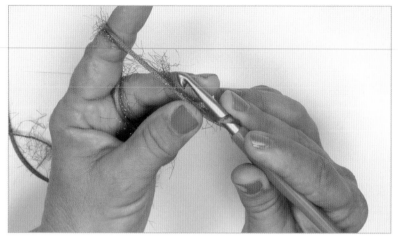

1 Take one strand of Rattail together with one strand of yarn.

2 Start with chain 4.

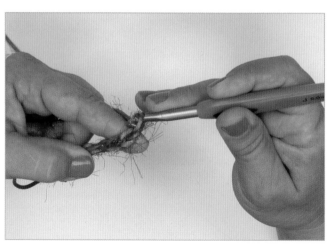

3 Chain 4.

4 Insert needle through first chain.

5 Pull thread through both loops to form a ring (circle). Slipstitch is completed.

6 Single crochet in each chain around the ring (circle).

7 Continue around until the lei is the length you want. For a regular lei, length should be 36 to 40 inches.

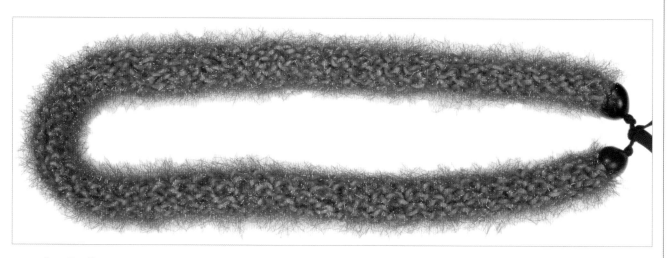

8 See Ending Your Lei on page 15 to complete the lei.

Finishing Your Lei

These instructions show you how to finish your lei. This is applicable to all five patterns.

After twisting your lei, you can fluff it so it looks fuller. Just take your lei and shake it. This can be done at anytime.

1 Take the middle of the lei in your left hand and twist the right side with your right hand going clockwise.

2 Then turn the lei, take the right side in your left hand, and do the same as above.

3 To tie off your ends, take the two yarns and tie a knot. Take the next two yarns and tie a knot. Do the same for the last two yarns and cut off ends as close to stitches as possible. This prevents your lei from accidentally coming apart.

1 Push back stitches on lei until you have 2 inches of line you crocheted on.

Supplies Needed:
2 kukui nuts (color of your choice)
5/8-inch satin or grosgrain ribbon
15-inch needle and thread
Big-eyed needle
A pair of pliers (optional)
Clear nail polish

These instructions show you how to finish your lei. There are other ways of ending lei. This is my way of ending and securing the lei so that it won't fall apart, and it looks neat.

2 Split ribbons to make an opening.

3 Take 5/8-inch ribbon and pull through opening.

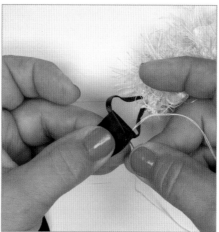

4 Fold edge of ribbon slightly.

5 Put a few hand stitches through ribbon to secure the lei.

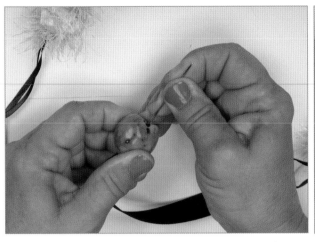 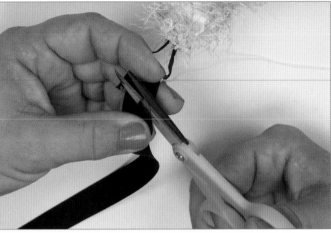

6 Put kukui nut on ribbon. If you use a big needle, it may fit through the kukui nut. If not, use pliers to pull the needle through. There's no right or wrong way (top or bottom) for you to put your kukui nut on the ribbon.

7 Push the thread and adjust the lei down to both ends after the kukui nut is on. Tie a knot at the end of the nut to secure it in place (both ends).

8 This secures the nut. Do this to both ends. Go back to Step 1 and repeat on the other side.

 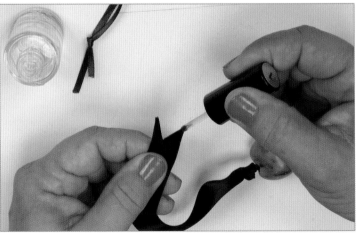

9 Snip the ribbon at both ends.

10 Apply clear nail polish so that the ribbon does not fray.

LEI
INSTRUCTIONS

Bougainvillea

Supplies Needed

- Olive Mustache
- Olive 1/8-inch ribbon
- Purple mustache
- Bouquet (fizz) whiskers
- Magenta mustache
- Floral (fizz) whiskers

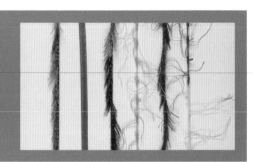

Instructions

Use instructions for Lei Pattern #1

Row 1. Olive mustache w/ Olive ribbon
Row 2. Purple mustache w/ Bouquet (fizz) whiskers
Row 3. Magenta mustache w/ Floral (fizz) whiskers

Bozu

Supplies Needed

- White chenille
- Mauve chenille
- Purple chenille

Instructions

Use instructions for Lei Pattern #1

Row 1. White chenille
Row 2. Mauve chenille
Row 3. Purple chenille

Cherries Jubilee

Supplies Needed

- Cherry eyebrow
- Red aquarius
- Olive eyebrow
- Green aquarius
- Pele's hair (shadow fizz)

Instructions

Use instructions for Lei Pattern #1

Row 1. Cherry eyebrow w/ Red aquarius
Row 2. Olive eyebrow w/ Green aquarius
Row 3. Pele's hair w/ Olive eyebrow

Cigar Lei

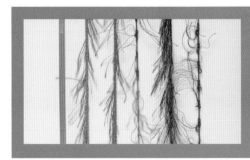

Supplies Needed

- Orange 1/8-inch ribbon
- Rust eyebrow
- Red eyebrow
- Flame (fizz) whiskers
- Brown & Tan mix mustache
- Brown (fizz) whiskers

Instructions

Use instructions for Lei Pattern #1

Row 1. Orange ribbon w/ Rust eybrow
Row 2. Red eyebrow w/ Flame (fizz)
        whiskers
Row 3. Brown & Tan mix mustache w/
        Brown (fizz) whiskers

Graduation Lei

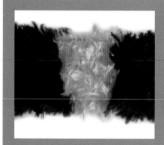

Supplies Needed

- 2 (primary color of school) boa
- 1 (secondary color of school) boa
(Refer to page 33 for Hawai'i High
School and College School Colors.)

Instructions

Use instructions for Lei Pattern #3

Row 1. First color 50 loops
Row 2. Second color 25 loops

Greens with Pīkake

Supplies Needed

- 1/8-inch Ivory ribbon
- 1/8-inch White ribbon
- Green eyebrow
- Green mustache (any color green can be used)

Instructions

Use instructions for Lei Pattern #1

Row 1. 1/8-inch Ivory ribbon w/ 1/8-inch
        White ribbon
Row 2. Green eyebrow w/ Green mustache
Row 3. Green eyebrow w/ Green mustache

Hinahina

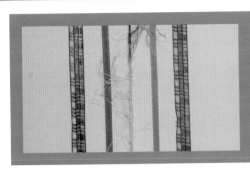

Supplies Needed

- Green aquarius
- Olive 1/8-inch ribbon
- Pele's hair (fizz)
- Gray 1/8-inch ribbon
- Black aquarius

Instructions

Use instructions for Lei Pattern #1

Row 1. Green aquarius w/ Olive 1/8-inch ribbon

Row 2. Pele's hair (fizz) w/ Gray 1/8-inch ribbon

Row 3. Pele's hair (fizz) w/ Black aquarius

Hinahina (Braided)

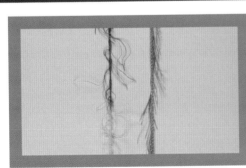

Supplies Needed

- Pele's hair (fizz shadow)
- Gray eyebrow

Instructions

Use instructions for Lei Pattern #2

Row 1. Pele's hair (fizz shadow) w/ Gray eyebrow

Honohono

Supplies Needed

- Delphinium (fizz) whiskers
- Olive eyebrow
- Pink & Blue gatto
- Mix Gray chenille

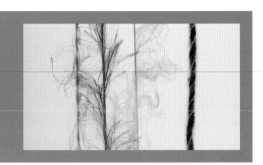

Instructions

Use instructions for Lei Pattern #1

Row 1. Delphinium (fizz) whiskers w/ Olive eyebrow

Row 2. Pink & Blue gatto w/ Olive eyebrow

Row 3. Mix Gray chenille (alone)

Marlene's Christmas Lei

Supplies Needed

- Red Rattail cord
- Red Shiny Matical yarn (cellophane)

Instructions

Use instructions for Lei Pattern #5

Row 1. Red Rattail cord together w/ Shiny Matical yarn (cellophane),or color of your choice

Mixed Rosettes

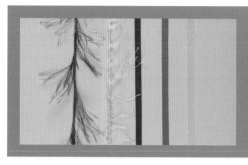

Supplies Needed

- Olive eyebrow
- Sherbert (fizz) whisker
- Maroon 1/8-inch ribbon
- Red 1/8-inch ribbon
- Pink 1/8-inch ribbon
(Or, colors of your choice)

Instructions

Use instructions for Lei Pattern #4

Row 1. Olive eyebrow w/ Sherbert (fizz) whiskers
Row 2. Maroon 1/8-inch ribbon
Row 3. Red 1/8-inch ribbon
Row 4. Pink 1/8-inch ribbon

Mokihana

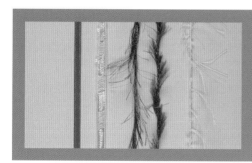

Supplies Needed

- Olive 1/8-inch ribbon
- Green carisso
- Olive eyebrow
- Olive mustache
- Lettuce (fizz) whiskers

Instructions

Use instructions for Lei Pattern #1

Row 1. Olive 1/8-inch ribbon w/ Green carisso
Row 2. Olive eyebrow w/ Olive mustache
Row 3. Olive mustache w/ Lettuce (fizz) whiskers

'Ohai Ali'i (Orange)

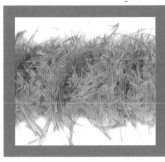

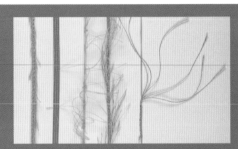

Supplies Needed

- Orange mustache
- Orange 1/8-inch ribbon
- Peach eyebrow
- Orange eyebrow
- Orange eyelash

Instructions

Use instructions for Lei Pattern #1

Row 1. Orange mustache w/ Orange 1/8-inch ribbon
Row 2. Peach eyebrow w/ Orange eyebrow
Row 3. Orange eyebrow w/ Orange eyelash

'Ohai Ali'i with Yellow Lehua

Supplies Needed

- Yellow 1/8-inch ribbon
- Yellow eyebrow
- Flame (fizz) whiskers
- Red eyebrow
- Red eyelash

Instructions

Use instructions for Lei Pattern #5

Row 1. Yellow 1/8-inch ribbon w/ Yellow eyebrow
Row 2. Flame (fizz) whiskers w/ Red eyebrow
Row 3. Flame (fizz) whiskers w/ Red eyelash

Ōlaʻa Beauty

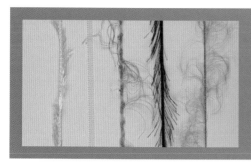

Supplies Needed

- Yellow mustache
- White 1/8-inch ribbon
- Delphinium (fizz) whiskers
- Navy eyebrow
- Purple voila

Instructions

Use instructions for Lei Pattern #4

Row 1. Yellow mustache w/ White
        1/8-inch ribbon
Row 2. Purple voila w/ Navy eyebrow
Row 3. Navy eyebrow w/ Delphinium
        (fizz) whiskers

Orchid with Pīkake

Supplies Needed

- Off-white 1/8-inch ribbon
- White 1/8-inch ribbon
- Purple eyebrow
- Purple mustache

Instructions

Use instructions for Lei Pattern #1

Row 1. Off-white 1/8-inch ribbon w/
        White 1/8-inch ribbon
Row 2. Purple mustache w/ Purple
        eyebrow
Row 3. Purple mustache w/ Purple
        eyebrow

Pakalana

Supplies Needed

- Moss Green eyebrow
- Gold Brown
- Brazilia #0074 eyebrow

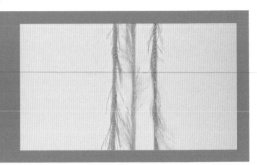

Instructions

Use instructions for Lei Pattern #2

Row 1. Crochet all 3 threads together and follow instructions for Lei Pattern #2

Pīkake with Marbella

Supplies Needed

- White carisso
- Ivory 1/8-inch ribbon
- Mauve marbella
- Mauve 1/8-inch ribbon
- Olive mustache
- Olive eyebrow

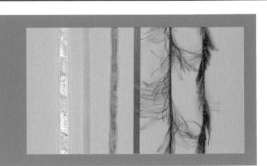

Instructions

Use instructions for Lei Pattern #1

Row 1. White carisso w/ Ivory 1/8-inch ribbon
Row 2. Mauve marbella w. Mauve 1/8-inch ribbon
Row 3. Olive mustache w/ Olive eyebrow

Pua 'Ōlena

Supplies Needed

- Cherry eyebrow
- Off-white eyebrow
- Light Yellow eyebrow
- Light Olive eyebrow
- White carisso
- Off-white 1/8-inch ribbon

Instructions

Use instructions for Lei Pattern #1

Row 1. Cherry Eyebrow w/ Off-white eyebrow

Row 2. Light Yellow eyebrow w/ Light Olive eyebrow

Row 3. White carisso w/ Off-white 1/8-inch ribbon

Purple Cigar

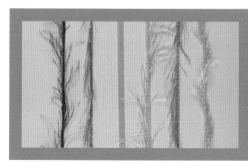

Supplies Needed

- Dark Purple eyebrow
- Medium Purple eyebrow
- Lavender 1/8-inch ribbon
- Lavender eyebrow
- Gray eyebrow
- Gray mustache

Instructions

Use instructions for Lei Pattern #1

Row 1. Dark Purple eyebrow w/ Medium Purple eyebrow

Row 2. Lavender 1/8-inch ribbon w/ Lavender eyebrow

Row 3. Gray eyebrow w/ Gray mustache

Red Lehua

Supplies Needed

- Red eyebrow
- Red flame (fizz) whiskers
- Red voila

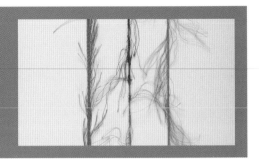

Instructions

Use instructions for Lei Pattern #2

Row 1. Red eyebrow w/ Flame (fizz) whiskers

Row 2. Flame (fizz) whiskers w/ Flame (fizz) whiskers

Row 3. Flame fizz (whiskers) w/ Red voila

Red & Yellow Lehua

Supplies Needed

- Olive 1/8-inch ribbon
- Olive mustache
- Red mustache
- Flame (fizz) whiskers
- Yellow mustache
- Sherbert (fizz) whiskers

Instructions

Use instructions for Lei Pattern #1

Row 1. Olive 1/8-inch ribbon w/ Olive mustache

Row 2. Red mustache w/ Flame (fizz) whiskers

Row 3. Yellow mustache w/ Sherbert (fizz) whiskers

Sea Shells

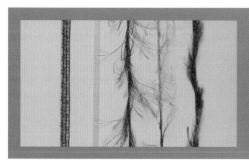

Supplies Needed

- Tan Aquarius
- Ivory 1/8-inch ribbon
- Olive eyebrow
- Earth (fizz) whiskers
- Olive mustache

Instructions

Use instructions for Lei Pattern #1

Row 1. Tan aquarius w/ Ivory 1/8-inch ribbon
Row 2. Olive eyebrow w/ Earth (fizz) whiskers
Row 3. Olive eyebrow w/ Olive mustache

Yellow Lehua with Pīkake

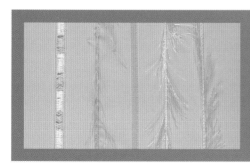

Supplies Needed

- Yellow carisso
- Sherbert (fizz) whiskers
- Off-white 1/8-inch ribbon
- White eyebrow
- Off-white eyebrow

Instructions

Use instructions for Lei Pattern #1

Row 1. Yellow carisso w/ Sherbert (fizz) whiskers
Row 2. Off-white 1/8-inch ribbon w/ White eyebrow
Row 3. Off-white 1/8-inch ribbon w/ Off-white Eyebrow

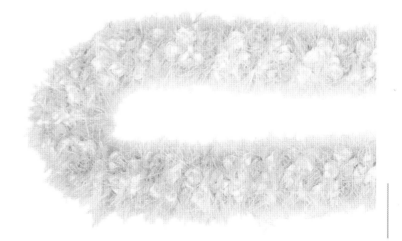

Headband Instructions

Supplies Needed:
1 headband
2 threads of your choice
1 ribbon of your choice
K hook or hook of your choice
Hot glue gun

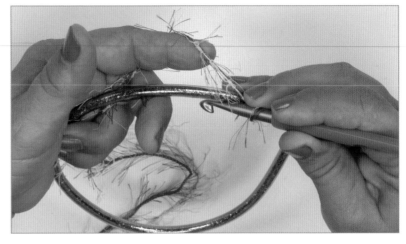

1 Take 2 threads and begin by single crocheting on a headband.

2 Single crochet and chain 3 on headband.

3 Repeat until you reach the other side of the band.

4 Turn, single crochet and chain 3 on the other half of the band.

5 Repeat in between the loops until the end of the row.

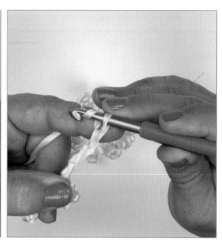

6 3rd Row: Single crochet and chain 4. Go back and single crochet in the 3rd chain from hook. Then single crochet in the last chain.

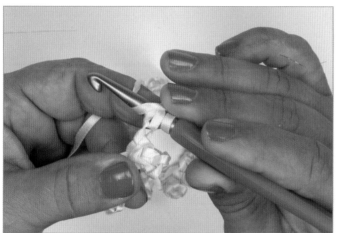

7 Repeat until you have covered the top of the headband.

8 Glue rosettes in middle of crocheted headband (hot glue). Trim off all ends.

Scrunchies

Supplies needed:
Ponytail rubber band
Leftover yarns and ribbons

Crochet scrunchies like making Lei Pattern #1. But, instead of using a lead line, use a ponytail rubber band. Crochet on the rubber band in a circle. This is another way of using your leftover yarns and ribbons.

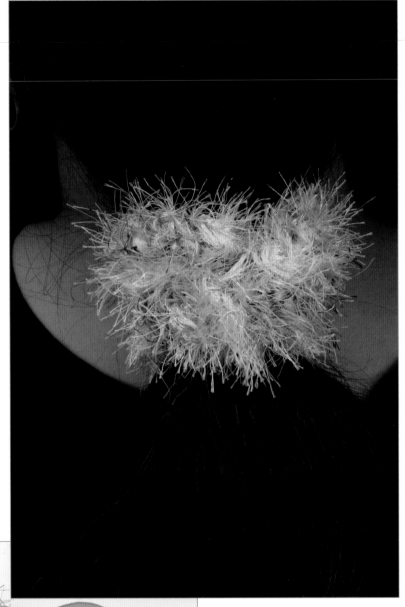

High School

O'ahu

Academy of the Pacific	Blue and White
'Aiea	Green and White
Ānuenue	Teal and Blue
Assets	Red, White and Royal Blue
Campbell	Orange and Black
Castle	Maroon, Gold, and White
Damien	Purple and Gold
Education Lab	Green and White
Farrington	Maroon and White
Hakipu'u Learning Center	Black and Gold
Hālau Kū Mana	Brown and Green
Hālau Lōkahi	Blue and White
Hanalani	Purple and Gold
Hawaii Baptist Academy	Black, Gold, and White
Hawaiian Mission Academy	Blue and White
'Iolani	Red, Black and White
Kahuku	Red and White
Kailua	Blue and White
Kaimukī	Green and Gold
Kaiser	Gold and Blue
Kalāheo	Orange and Blue
Kalani	Red and White
Kamehameha	Royal Blue and White
Kapolei	Teal, Black, and Gold
Kea'au	Navy Blue and Red
Ke Kula 'o Samuel M. Kamakau Lab	Royal Blue
Lanikila Baptist	Red, White, and Blue
La Pietra	Royal Blue & Powder Blue
Leilehua	Green and Gold
Le Jardin	Blue and White
Lutheran	Navy Blue and White
Maryknoll	Maroon and Gold
McKinley	Black and Gold
Mid—Pacific Institute	Green and White
Mililani	Brown and Gold
Moanalua	Royal Blue and Silver Gray
Myron B. Thompson Academy	Royal Blue and Silver
Nānākuli	Black and Gold
Pacific Buddhist Academy	Green, Purple, and Gold
Pearl City	Purple and White
Punahou	Buff and Blue
Radford	Red, Black, and White
Roosevelt	Red and Gold

Hawai'i High School and College School Colors

Use this list as a reference for crochet Lei Pattern #3: The Graduation Lei.

Hawai'i School Colors

Sacred Hearts Academy   .White and Gold
St. Andrew's Priory . . . . . .Red and White
St. Francis . . . . .Blue and White
St. Louis . . . . .Red and Blue
Varsity . . . . .Blue and White
Waialua . . . . .Scarlet and Gray
Wai'anae . . . . .Red and Blue
Waipahu . . . . .Blue and Gold
Waldorf . . . . .Blue and White

Big Island

Hawai'i Academy of Arts & Science   .Blue
                                    and Silver
Hawai'i Preparatory Academy . . . . . .Red
                                  and White
Hilo . . . . .Blue and Gold
Honoka'a . . . . .Green and Gold
Kanu 'o Ka Āina . . . . .changes each year
Ka'ū . . . . .Maroon and White
Kealakehe . . . . . . .Blue, White, and Silver
Ke Ana La'ahana . . .Navy Blue and White
Kohala . . . . .Black and Gold
Konawaena . . . . .Green and White
Laupāhoehoe . . . . .Blue and Gold
Pāhoa . . . . .Green and White
Parker . . . . . . .Black, White, and Maroon
St. Joseph . . . . .Red and Gold
Waiākea . . . . .Royal Blue and White
Waters of Life . . . . . . .check with school
West Hawai'i Explorations Academy .Dark
                          Green and Silver

Maui, Moloka'i, Lāna'i

Baldwin . . . . .Maroon and Blue
Hāna . . . . .Green and Gold
Kīhei New Century . . .Orange and Black
King Kekaulike . . . . .Black and Teal
Lāna'i . . . . .Green and Gold
Maui . . . . .Royal Blue and White
Moloka'i . . . . .Green and White
St. Anthony . . . . .Blue and Gold
Seabury Hall . . . . .Red and Blue

Kaua'i and Ni'ihau

Ipu Ha'a Academy of Natural Sciences . . . . .Green
                                    and Maroon
Kapa'a . . . . .Green and White
Kaua'i . . . . .Red and White
Ke Kula Ni'ihau 'o Kekaha . . . . .Gold and White
Waimea . . . . .Blue and White
Ni'ihau . . . . .Purple, White, and Lavender
Ni'ihau School of Kekaha . . . . .check with school

Colleges and Universities

Brigham Young–Hawai'i . . . .Crimson, Gold, and Gray
Chaminade . . . . .Royal Blue and white
Hawai'i Community College . . . . .Maroon and White
Hawai'i Pacific University . . . . .Columbia Blue and
                                      Kelly Green
Heald's Business College . . . . .Blue and Gold
Honolulu Community College . . . . . .Blue and Yellow
Kapi'olani Community College . .Royal Blue and White
Kaua'i Community College . . . . .Green and Gold
Leeward Community College . . . . . .Purple and Gold
Maui Community College . . . . .Blue and Green
UH-Hilo . . . . .Red, White, and Royal Blue
UH-Mañoa . . . . .Green and White
UH-West O'ahu . . . . .Teal and White
Windward Community College . . . . .Forest Green

Other "How to" books by Mutual Publishing

Hawaiian Tropical Flower Arranging: A Step-By-Step Guide

By Laurie Shimizu Ide

The best-selling "How-To" books author shares her expertise as a long-time florist to present 32 classic contemporary flower arrangement designs easy enough for a beginner.

Hawaiian Lei Making Step-By-Step Guide

By Laurie Shimizu Ide

The Hawaiian Lei Making Step-by-Step Guide is everything you'd ever want to know about lei making! A complete photographic instruction guide & reference tool to over 50 major flowers and plants used in making Hawaiian lei.

Hawaiian Seed Lei Making Step-By-Step Guide

By Laurie Shimizu Ide

An authoratative guide to this popular local craft. With colorful pictures, simple step-by-step instructions, and helpful tips, you too can become a seed-lei crafter in no time!

How to Make Hawaiian Ribbon Leis: A Step-By-Step Guide

By Jim Widess

Step by step photographic process to make 15 ribbon leis.

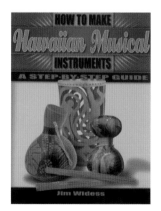

How to Make Hawaiian Musical Instruments: A Step-By-Step Guide

By Jim Widess

Step-by-step photographic process to make 18 traditional instruments.

Poakalani Hawaiian Quilt Cushion Patterns & Designs Volume I and Volume II

By Poakalani and John Serrao

Fifteen original block patterns and designs for both the experienced and beginning quilter. Includes easy-to-follow how-to photographs illustrating: folding material and cutting the design, appliqué, preparation before quilting, quilting techniques, quilting styles, quilting block samples and many more helpful hints for the beginning quilter!

Poakalani Hawaiian Quilt Cushion Patterns & Designs Volume IV

By Poakalani and John Serrao

Fifteen new quilt patterns, includes how-to photographs.

Poakalani Hawaiian Quilt Cushion Patterns & Designs Volume III

By Poakalani and John Serrao

More quilt patterns guaranteed to please quilters everywhere.

MUTUAL PUBLISHING

To order, visit our website
www.mutualpublishing.com